Remarkable Reptiles

Complete Theme Unit With Fascinating Facts & Awesome Activities
That Teach About Lizards, Crocodiles, Turtles, Snakes & More!

by Robin Bernard

SCHOLASTIC
PROFESSIONAL BOOKS

New York • Toronto • London • Auckland • Sydney • Mexico City • New Dehli • Hong Kong

Dedication

For Jerry — one more time

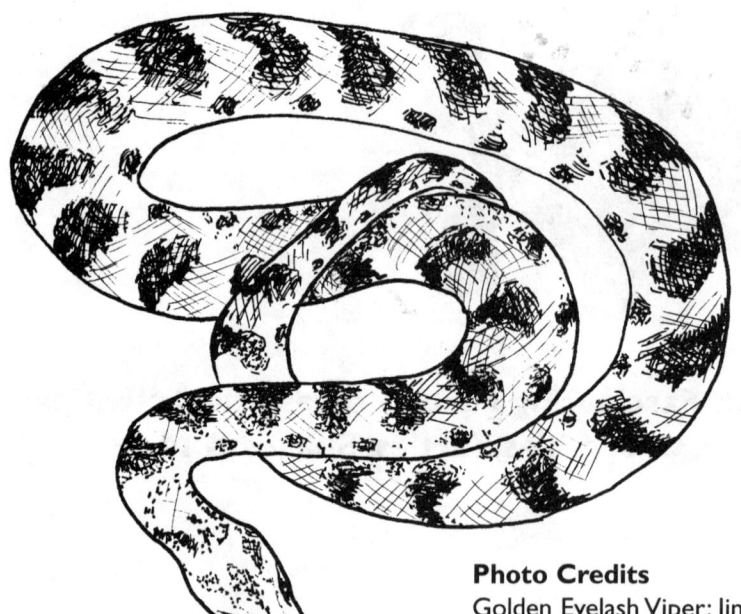

Cover design
by **Norma Ortiz**

Interior and poster design
by **Holly Grundon**

Interior illustrations
by **Robin Bernard** and
Kathie Kelleher

Photo research
by **Sarah Longacre**

Photo Credits
Golden Eyelash Viper: Jim Battles/Dembinsky Photo Associates

Yacare Caiman: Fritz Polking/Dembinsky Photo Associates

Green Sea Turtle: Eric Haucke/Gregory Ochocki Productions/Photo Researchers Inc.

Panther Chameleon: Martin Harvey/Photo Researchers Inc.

ISBN 0-439-11764-X
Copyright © 2001 by Robin Bernard
All rights reserved.
Printed in the U.S.A.

Scholastic Inc. grants teachers permission to photocopy the activity sheets from this book for classroom use. No other part of this publication may be reproduced in whole or in part, or stored in a retrieval system, or transmitted in any form or by any means, electronic, mechanical, photocopying, recording, or otherwise, without written permission of the publisher. For information regarding permission, write to Scholastic Inc., 555 Broadway, New York, NY 10012.

Contents

How to Use This Book 4

Background Information 5

Student Activities 10
    What Kind of Animal Am I? *(Science, Critical Thinking, Math)* . . . 10
    Resemble a Reptile *(Science, Math)* 10
    A Snake of Your Own *(Science, Language Arts, Art)* 11
    Ask Albert *(Science, Art)* 12
    Sea Turtle's Baby Book *(Math, Language Arts, Science)* 13
    Large-as-Life Python *(Math, Art, Cooperative Learning)* 14
    Reptile Fact Cards *(Science Math, Research Skills)* 15
    Tortoise Talk *(Language Arts, Art)* 16
    Komodo Dragons & Mice *(Crafts, Language Arts)* 17
    Daily Reptile Reporter *(Science, Critical Thinking)* 18
    Teaching With the Poster *(Mapping Skills, Critical Thinking)* 18

Student Reproducible Pages 19

Reptile Resources 32

Poster: "A World of Reptiles" . . . . *bound in the book*

How To Use This Book

Talk about scaly, slithery reptiles and you may hear shrieks of both "yuck!" and "cool!" This book is designed to allow both camps to safely explore the world of snakes, crocodiles, lizards, and turtles—from their history to their astounding adaptations as predators and prey—and turn any trepidation to wonder.

Easing In and Wrapping Up

Before starting the unit, ask children what they think of snakes, lizards, crocodiles, and turtles. A little information can dispel any apprehension your students may have.

Create a KWL chart. Divide a large sheet of butcher paper into three columns. Invite students to fill the first column with facts they already **Know** about reptiles. For the second column, ask students what they **Want** to find out about reptiles—for example, why do snakes seem to stare? Revisit the chart at the end of the unit and encourage students to share what they've **Learned** about reptiles. Ask students if their feelings toward reptiles have changed.

Picking and Choosing Activities

Select the activities in this book that will best stimulate and satisfy your students' curiosity. To meet the needs of the children, feel free to change and adapt the activities, or use them to launch spin-off projects. Check the "Keep Going" section at the end of activities for extension ideas.

Using the Poster

Use the poster to launch discussions about reptiles and their habitats. Students can add to the poster by doing more research on the species shown. They can also research reptiles that live in other parts of the world. Invite them to tack a picture and description of their species to the poster in the appropriate spot.

Reading About Reptiles

Books will give your students a chance to meet even more reptiles. Put together a collection of fiction and nonfiction books and set aside time for reading. Look for "Book Breaks" at the end of each activity and "Reptile Resources" at the back of the book.

Reptile Romp

By sharing what they've learned about reptiles, kids can cement their knowledge and help other children become less fearful of these animals. Invite friends and family for a Reptile Romp and enjoy the fruits of the various activities in this book. For treats, try gummy alligators, chocolate "turtles," and licorice "thread snakes." Ask a local expert from a nearby zoo or pet shop to bring in live reptiles for the children to meet.

Background Information

What Is a Reptile?

These creepy critters come in so many shapes and sizes, it may be difficult to understand why scientists group a snake and a turtle together. Here are the minimum requirements for entry into the reptile club:

BACKBONE — All reptiles are *vertebrates*, which means they have a central spine that supports a skeleton.

SCALES — All reptiles have scales (or plates, in the case of turtles) that prevent them from losing moisture through their skin. That's why many reptiles thrive in deserts, where few other forms of life can survive. Scales are made mostly of *keratin*—a material that's found in our fingernails and toenails. This armor also helps protect reptiles from injury.

COLD-BLOODED BODY — Reptiles, as well as amphibians and fish, are *cold-blooded*. That means their body temperature changes with the outside temperature. (Mammals are *warm-blooded*—they maintain constant body temperatures.)

When exposed to temperature extremes, reptiles have ways to keep from freezing or overheating. For example, they burrow under the ground to escape both sun and cold, or sunbathe to warm up.

LUNGS — All reptiles, even sea snakes, breathe air through lungs.

EGGS — Except for a few types of snakes and lizards, most reptiles lay eggs. Unlike aquatic reptiles, land-dwelling reptiles lay eggs with hard shells to keep the embryo from drying out. Baby snakes and lizards come equipped with a sharp egg tooth to break through their shells. Crocodiles and tortoises have a horny knob on the end of their snouts that serve the same purpose.

IT'S A FACT!

For warm-blooded animals, holding a constant body temperature requires a lot of food for energy. Cold-blooded reptiles, on the other hand, can go without eating for weeks or even months!

Remarkable Reptiles

The Early Years

More than 300 million years ago, reptiles evolved from *amphibians*, animals that live partly in water and partly on land.

When dinosaurs died out 65 million years ago, many types of reptiles became extinct as well. This mass extinction may have been caused by a meteorite that slammed into Earth. Reptile species that survived the catastrophe evolved to become the four groups we know today: (1) turtles; (2) crocodilians; (3) snakes and lizards; and (4) the tuatara—a rare group that remains almost exactly as it was 200 million years ago!

Tough Turtles

Turtles are the only reptiles protected by a bony shell. There are about 250 species of turtles, including land-based tortoises and water-dwelling terrapins. Of these, about 200 species live in and around water.

These hard-shelled animals range in size from 4-inch bog turtles to 6-foot-long leatherbacks. They can be found in oceans, forests, and deserts. If you want to know where a turtle spends its time, check out its feet. Semiaquatic species are likely to have webbed toes. Aquatic species have flippers instead of feet.

Still, all turtles share many adaptations. Although turtles can't hear well, they have a sharp sense of smell and excellent vision that lead them to their meals, which are made up mainly of plants, fish, and shellfish. The toothless creatures tear off bites with powerful, sharp-edged "beaks." Carnivorous species have sharp, hooked beaks to hold prey.

Most turtles use their strong beaks to inflict nasty bites on enemies. Of course, their tough shells offer a quick and handy refuge, so turtles have no need for speed.

To escape from temperature extremes, tortoises spend hot days in burrows and crawl out at night. They may also sleep through the hot weather, just as cold-dwelling species hibernate in winter. For a winter sleep, turtles bury themselves in mud, often at the bottom of a pond. They can go for long periods without breathing, and some have adaptations such as an elongated "snorkel" for a nose.

All turtles, including sea turtles, lay their eggs on land. After laying their eggs, mother turtles leave and never look back. The eggs are incubated by the sun's warmth or by the heat of rotting vegetation, and the young receive no parental care. The nest's temperature determines the sex of the hatchlings:

IT'S A FACT!

To get food, the alligator snapping turtle waits at the bottom of the lake and wiggles the wormlike tip of its tongue. When a fish swims over to investigate, the turtle quickly snaps up the unsuspecting fish!

a higher temperature produces more females. Very few of the baby turtles make it to adulthood—most fall prey to birds or other animals. But those that make it may live a long time. The oldest reptile on record is a 152-year-old Marion's tortoise.

Today, habitat loss, overcollection, pollution, disease, competition from and predation by invader species threaten the existence of about one third of turtle species. Around the world, people are working to save endangered turtles and their habitats.

Crafty Crocodilians

Members of this animal family range in size from the 4-foot dwarf crocodile to the 25-foot saltwater crocodile. Alligators range from 7 to 15 feet and can weigh more than 1,300 pounds. Under the skin, crocodilians are covered with plates, called *scutes*, which protect them from drying out. Though slow and awkward on land, 'gators and crocs are powerful swimmers.

How can you tell the difference between a crocodile and an alligator? Take a close look at their jaws. (Not too close!) Crocodiles have triangular-shaped snouts and both rows of teeth, top and bottom, are visible when their mouths are closed. Alligators have broad, flat heads with rounded snouts. In a closed mouth, only the upper teeth stick out.

Alligators and crocodiles are carnivorous—they eat meat. Adults can devour animals as large as a zebra! One relative, the shy gharial of northern India, eats strictly fish.

As they tear into their food, crocodilians often lose teeth. But unlike people, they can grow as many new ones as they need. A half-grown crocodile may already be on its 45th set!

Their strength and ferocity protect crocodilians from predators—except for humans, who hunt them for their skins. Left alone, alligators may live 50 years, and crocodiles even longer.

Today, most crocodilian species are protected by strict laws. Loss of habitat is still the biggest danger to the species today.

Leaping Lizards!

Lizards range in size from 1 1/2 inches to the 18-foot-long Salvador monitor lizard. More than 3,750 known lizard species can be found in warm spots around the globe.

> **IT'S A FACT!**
> To keep water from entering their snouts, crocodiles shut their nostrils before they dive.

> **IT'S A FACT!**
> Crocodiles have a surprising system of dental care. Feathered "toothpicks"—small birds called plovers—hop from tooth to tooth in the crocodile's open mouth, pecking out leftovers stuck between the teeth.

Remarkable Reptiles 7

While it's true that lizards can leap, they have more innovative methods of movement. Scaly toes provide enough friction for scampering up walls, while round toes act as suction cups for trips across the ceiling. Some species are super swimmers. The draco lizard spreads wing-like membranes to catch the air as it glides from tree to tree, and the basilisk lizard can run across water!

Fleeing is just one way lizards avoid being eaten by predators. If an animal grabs a lizard by the tail, for instance, the tail breaks off easily. It eventually grows back. Chameleons change colors to blend into their surroundings and hide from enemies. Two species, the Gila monster and the Mexican beaded lizard, are poisonous.

To detect enemies and prey, lizards use their tongues to pick up traces of chemicals in order to "smell" or "taste" their surroundings. Tongues serve other purposes as well. Some types of geckos stretch out their tongue to clean their eyeballs, and many lizards shoot out long, sticky-tipped tongues to grab insects.

Slithery Snakes

Snakes are "newcomers" among reptiles, having been around for only 100 million years. But in that time, 2,700 species have evolved—from the tiny thread snake (about the size of the lead in a pencil) to the 33-foot-long, 300-pound anaconda.

Most snakes are small, harmless to humans, and helpful in controlling rodent populations. So why are they so feared and disliked? Is it their slithery motion? How else could animals with no legs get around? Is it the myth that they're slimy? Actually, snakes are cool and smooth to the touch. Maybe it's their unblinking stare. But snakes can't help that—they have no eyelids! Transparent scales protect their eyes and keep them moist. When snakes molt, they shed this layer along with the rest of their skin.

Although snakes have fairly good vision, they are deaf. They usually detect prey by "tasting" the air with their flickering tongue, which picks up trace amounts of chemicals the way our nose does to smell.

Snakes called pit vipers can sense their prey's body heat in the dark. A pit between each nostril and eye can detect the heat radiating from other animals. The viper then strikes and injects venom through their hollow fangs!

Some snakes kill their prey by biting, with or without venom. Other snakes grab their prey with

IT'S A FACT!
Chameleons can move their eyes in different directions at the same time to spot fast-buzzing insects.

IT'S A FACT!
The horned toad lizard has an amazing defense: When threatened, it squirts blood from its eye to scare away (or gross out) its attacker.

IT'S A FACT!
Unlike most snakes, rattlesnakes don't lay eggs. All 29 species give birth to live young.

8 Remarkable Reptiles

> **IT'S A FACT!**
>
> Most snakes drink water from puddles or ponds, but some soak in water through their skin.

their teeth, then coil their body around the animal and squeeze until it suffocates—a process called *constriction*. Very few constrictors are large enough to put the squeeze on humans, and only one, the South American anaconda, is found anywhere near us.

Snakes swallow their prey whole, by unhinging their jaws. After swallowing their prey, they squiggle and squirm to help push the big meal into their stomachs. Digestive juices slowly break down the meal. Since most snakes aren't more than a couple of feet long, their diets usually consist of amphibians, insects, and small mammals, such as mice and rats. Some snakes are specialists, however. There are those that eat eggs almost exclusively, while others eat only snails. King cobras can swallow poisonous snakes—they're immune to the poison.

Surprisingly, snake venom can also save lives. Venom may be used to make an antidote to its own poisonous effects. Viper venom is also used in medications that treat high blood pressure, heart failure, kidney failure, and hemophilia.

Tuatara—In a Class by Itself

This rare, ancient reptile has crept its way through more than 200 million years nearly unchanged. Found only on the small coastal islands of New Zealand, these 2-pound, 2-foot-long reptiles bear a Maori name that means "peaks along the back."

Unlike real lizards, this lizard look-alike doesn't have ears. But it has an extra row of upper teeth. Its lower teeth fit neatly between the two rows. This prehistoric animal also possesses a third eye in the middle of its head. Covered with a layer of skin, this eye contains a retina, lens, and nerves like any other eye.

The tuatara doesn't do anything quickly. A ponderous metabolism means it creeps slowly and heavily. So its energy needs are low: The tuatara can survive on a few small insects a day, and at times, may go nearly an hour without breathing!

This lumbering animal can survive only on remote islands where it doesn't have to compete with speedy snakes, lizards, or other animals for food. Tuataras lived in other parts of New Zealand before Western settlers brought along their cats and pigs, which easily snatched up tuataras. Now the species thrives on a few small islands that are protected from these invaders.

Tuataras may live to be 100 years old. They start mating when they're about 20, and lay eggs that take up to about 15 months to hatch.

> **IT'S A FACT!**
>
> The tuatara lives in a burrow it shares with a bird—a petral or a shearwater. The night-hunting reptile sleeps there during the day, and the bird beds down at night!

Remarkable Reptiles

Student Activities

What Kind of Animal Am I?
(Science, Critical Thinking, Math)

Students classify animals based on their physical characteristics.

You'll Need

What Am I? Animal Maze (page 19)
- different colored crayons or markers

Divide the class into groups of three students. Make a copy of page 19 for each group. Have children look at the three animals on the page and read the information under each one. Ask: What kind of animal do you think is the frog? What about the monkey? The snake?

Provide each student in a group with a different color crayon. Invite one student to pick an animal and follow the maze to find out whether the animal is a reptile, amphibian, or mammal. When the student reaches a question, have him or her decide if the answer is yes or no. (Children can check their answers by referring back to the information written under the animal.) Have the other children in the group follow the same procedure using a different color crayon for the monkey and rattlesnake.

Answers

frog—amphibian; monkey—mammal; rattlesnake—reptile

Keep Going

List other animals on the board and challenge students to determine which group the animals belong to. For example, human, rabbit, alligator, wolf, iguana, lion, turtle, tortoise, cobra, toad, goat, and salamander.

Book Break

The Yucky Reptile Alphabet Book by Jerry Pallotta and Ralph Masiello (Charlesbridge Publishing, 1990). Find out why boa constrictors swallow their meals whole, why Gila monsters' tails are so fat, and more, in this beautiful, decidedly not-yucky book.

Resemble a Reptile
(Science, Math)

Students explore reptilian adaptations through simulation activities.

You'll Need

oaktag • paper • pencil • small mirror (optional) • cotton balls • scent (cologne or food extract) • 2 stopwatches • over-the-calf men's sock with the toe cut off (one per student in a group)

In this series of seven activities, children discover firsthand what it's like to be a reptile—while having fun! Set up seven reptile stations in the classroom (see instructions, page 11). Then copy each of the instructions on oaktag and post them in

Remarkable Reptiles

the appropriate stations.

Place paper and pencils in Stations 1, 2, and 4 for students to record their data. Before students enter the classroom, prepare for Station 6 by adding scent to cotton balls and hiding them in different places around the room. You may want to let students get a whiff of the scent before they try to find the hidden cotton balls. Station 7 requires students to slither on the floor. You may want to ask children to wear play clothes.

Have students count off by seven to form seven groups. Groups should start at the station with their same group number and move from station to station in numerical order.

STATION 1: Alligators have about 70 teeth and gharials have 100. How many do you have? Count your teeth by feeling them one by one or by looking in a mirror. Record that number on the data sheet.

STATION 2: Snakes can't blink because they have no eyelids. How long can you stare without blinking? Have a partner time you and record the time on the data sheet.

STATION 3: A gecko cleans its eyeballs with its tongue. Can you touch your nose with your tongue? Can your tongue touch the tip of your chin?

STATION 4: Slow-moving reptiles may breathe once per minute—or less! How many times do you breathe in one minute? Breathing naturally, count how many times you breathe while someone times a minute. Record the number on the data sheet.

STATION 5: Pull a cut off sock over your arm, from wrist to shoulder. Then try to "shed" your sock "skin" without using your hands!

STATION 6: Reptiles find food by following the scent of another animal. Can you sniff out the scented cotton balls in your classroom?

STATION 7: Crumple four pieces of scrap paper to use as "eggs." A mother python curls around her eggs and moves them with her body. Can you do that with your paper eggs?

Keep Going

Use the data from Stations 1, 2, and 4 to make bar graphs of the number of teeth in each group, the length of time students can go without blinking, and the number of breaths students take per minute.

Book Break

I Wonder Why Snakes Shed Their Skins and Other Questions About Reptiles by Amanda O'Neill (Kingfisher Books, 1996). Students can find the answers to those reptile questions they've always wondered about, and those they haven't thought of yet.

A Snake of Your Own
(Science, Language Arts, Art)

Students research their favorite snake and present their coolest finding to the class.

Remarkable Reptiles 11

You'll Need

Design a Snake (page 20) ◎ paste ◎ oaktag ◎ scissors ◎ crayons or markers ◎ pencil ◎ hole-punch ◎ string or yarn ◎ wire coat hangers (optional)

Give children time to browse through the nonfiction reptile books from the resource list (page 32), or help them find reptile information in the library. Ask each student to choose a favorite snake to write and talk about. Then have students make their favorite snake:

1. Make a photocopy of page 20 for each student. Have students cut out the label at the bottom of the page. Then, have them paste the rest of the page to oaktag and cut out the snake.
2. Have students color both sides of the shape to look like their favorite snake.
3. Have them write the snake's name on the label and add an interesting fact about the snake. Paste the label to the snake's belly.
4. Invite each student to introduce his or her snake to the class.

To display the snakes, punch a hole on each snake (vary the hole's placement from snake to snake). Display the slithery bunch by suspending them from the ceiling using yarn or string, or by assembling several mobiles using wire coat hangers and string.

Book Break

Extremely Weird Snakes by Sarah Lovett John (Muir Publications, 1996). Great photos and easy-to-digest information get you close to the strangest of slitherers, and show what's cool about more ordinary varieties.

Ask Albert
(Science, Art)

Constructing this paper alligator allows students to learn and communicate information.

You'll Need

Albert the Alligator (page 21) ◎ scissors ◎ paste ◎ oaktag ◎ pencil

Students will love being alligator experts as they create questions and answers for their very own alligator-shaped quiz cards. Invite children to browse through books on the resource list or other sources to find information about alligators. Then challenge students to come up with two short questions (and answers) for their quiz cards. You can also have them choose from a list of prepared questions such as these about the American alligator:

- How long do alligators live? *(50 years or more)*
- How big do alligators usually grow? *(About 6 to 12 feet)*
- How many eggs does an alligator lay? *(20–70)*
- What's one way for a baby alligator to travel? *("Piggy-backing" on its mom's back!)*

Follow the steps below to make an Ask Albert quiz card:

1. Make a copy of page 21 for each student. Have students cut out Albert the Alligator along the dotted lines and paste him to oaktag.
2. Help students carefully cut along the three dashed lines along Albert's back to form slots.
3. Cut out the "scutes" pattern and slide the tabs into the three slots on Albert's back. Fold and tape the tabs on the reverse side. Cut the scutes along the solid lines.
4. Have students write their questions on the blank scutes. Then have them write the answers behind the matching scute.

Invite students to use their Alberts to quiz one another. Suggest they take their Alberts home to stump their families!

Book Break

The Enormous Crocodile by Roald Dahl (Quentin Puffin, 1993). A most amazing crocodile in a muddy African river sets its sights on a fat, juicy little child in this classically creepy Roald Dahl story.

Sea Turtle's Baby Book
(Math, Language Arts, Science)

Students learn about the life of sea turtles as they use sequencing skills to put the pages of a story in order.

You'll Need

Sea Turtle Mini-Book (page 22)   scissors
construction paper   crayons
ribbon or yarn   hole-punch

Tell students that they'll make a mini-book about the only time sea turtles come ashore—when female turtles struggle up the beach to lay their eggs. Here's what to do:

1. Give each student a copy of page 22.
2. Have students cut the pages apart along the dashed lines. Challenge them to put the pages in sequential order so they can make a book.
3. Encourage students to color the pictures. Have them make a cover for their books using construction paper.
4. Help students punch a hole through the pages and tie them together with ribbon and yarn. Have them write their names and the title of the book on the cover.

Keep Going

Follow up this activity with a discussion on adaptation. Sea turtles have flippers, land turtles have separate toes, and turtles that split their time between water and land have webbed toes. Have students consider their own feet. For different activities and climates, people wear "adaptations" on their feet. Ask students: What do we put on our feet to help us walk in the snow? to skate? to play basketball? What kinds of footwear could help us climb a tree or walk in the desert?

Book Break

Into the Sea by Brenda Z. Guiberson (Henry Holt, 1996). Follow a sea turtle hatchling on its journey from egg to the sea and back to the same beach to lay eggs as an adult.

Large-as-Life Python
(Math, Art, Cooperative Learning)

Math meets science as students create a wriggling, life-size python the whole school can enjoy.

You'll Need

Python Patterns (page 23) ◎ oaktag
◎ ruler or yardstick ◎ scissors ◎ paste
◎ markers ◎ clear and masking tape
◎ brass fasteners ◎ hole-punch

Invite students to describe how a snake moves. Ask: Can humans and other animals move like that? Why do they think so? Tell students that snakes have spines that are made of as many as 300 small, linked bones called *vertebrae*. (Humans, on the other hand, have only 33 vertebrae.) Snakes wriggle so well by moving each of these bones in sequence. Ask: How do you think a big snake would move if it had only three or four long vertebrae?

Tell students that they will be creating a real-size, 33-foot-long "pet" python—as long as a school bus!—out of several 3-inch vertebrae. Here's how:

1. Begin by showing students how to measure 33 feet, marking the length at 1-foot intervals with masking tape. Then, show students what three inches looks like. Ask students: If we make the body 32 feet long (not including the head and tail), how many pieces do you think it will take to make the python? *(128. You might want to ask students to come up with different ways to calculate the number.)*

2. Make about 70 copies of page 23 to complete the python. (You actually need only 64 but it's best to have extras.) Give each student one copy at a time.

3. Have students paste the page to oaktag and color each pattern with brightly colored designs.

4. Help children cut out the patterns and tape the ends together to form circles. Punch holes through the circles on the rounded tabs. Use brass fasteners to connect the sections, as shown.

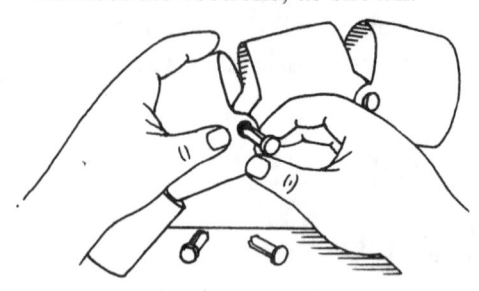

5. Have kids measure the snake after each new addition. You may want to set up a daily chart to record the snake's growing length each day.

6. When the snake is about 32 feet long, roll two pieces of construction paper

Remarkable Reptiles

into cone shapes—one for the head and one for the tail. Trim to fit, and tape them to the end sections, as illustrated. Draw eyes on the head and paste a paper tongue in the mouth. Take a class vote to name your pet. Let the students (carefully!) examine how the snake squiggles. Ask: How is it like a real snake?

Keep Going

Add poetic couplets to each section of the snake. Read the sample couplets below aloud and invite kids to think of descriptive reptile words that rhyme. Then challenge students to write their own couplets about any reptile. Have students copy them neatly onto 1 1/2- by 4-inch self-stick labels that can be affixed to the python.

I met a boa called "Rugby,"
Who really wanted to hug me!

That bulge in the rattlesnake's tummy
Was a gopher that tasted just yummy!

A turtle can stay alive and well
Just by hiding inside its shell.

Book Break

Verdi by Janell Cannon (Harcourt Brace, 1997). This bright, engaging picture book features Verdi, a young yellow python who's determined not to be a boring green adult.

Reptile Fact Cards
(Science, Math, Research Skills)

Students use research skills to create reptile fact cards, then sort them.

You'll Need

Reptile Fact Cards (pages 24–25) • scissors • construction paper • paste

Photocopy pages 24–25 for each student. For durability, have students paste the sheets to construction paper, then cut apart the cards along the dashed lines. Challenge the children to find more information about each reptile from your school library or the resource list. Have them write a fact or two about each animal in the space provided, then color in the animals. Invite children to share what they've discovered. Ask: Which reptiles do you think are the most interesting? the most dangerous? the funniest looking?

Explain to students that scientists organize the millions of animals in the world into groups. Animals with similar characteristics or attributes are grouped together. As a class, see how many different ways you can

Remarkable Reptiles

group the reptiles on the cards—for example, children could sort them by color, shells versus scales, legs versus no legs, etc. Inform students that scientists have sorted reptiles into five groups—turtle, crocodilian, lizard, snake, and tuatara—and have them sort the cards into five piles accordingly.

Keep Going

To play a game of "Reptile Concentration," cut along the dotted line to separate each animal's picture from its fact card. Have children shuffle the cards and place them facedown on a table or desk. Children play Concentration by turning over two cards at a time and trying to match a picture card with its fact card.

Book Break

Reptiles by Lois Ballard (Children's Press, 1982). More facts about these amazing animals presented in a format your students can understand.

Tortoise Talk
(Language Arts, Art)

Students get creative as they construct a paper turtle and write a story about it.

You'll Need

- A Turtle's Tale (page 26)
- oaktag
- paste
- scissors
- pencils
- markers or tempera paint and brushes
- 2 small paper plates (for each child)
- hole-punch
- yarn

Children will enjoy creating a story about a tortoise and assembling an unusual turtle book. Here's how:

1. Photocopy page 26 for each student. Have students paste the page to oaktag for durability, then cut out the turtle shape. Have students color the tortoise's head, feet, and tail, but not the round middle section.

2. Invite students to fill in the blanks to create a story about the tortoise. Let them be as silly as they want!

3. To create the tortoise's shell, have students turn a paper plate upside down and paint a design on it. Let it dry.

4. Place the second plate right side up. This is the bottom part of the shell. Lay the tortoise body on it and mark where the body touches the rim of the plate. Paste the marked areas and set the tortoise body on the plate so that they stick together.

5. Cover both the body and bottom shell with the painted shell. Punch two holes on the rim of both plates and tie the tortoise book together with pieces of yarn. Have children write their names on the underside of the bottom shell.

Remarkable Reptiles

Invite students to share their stories with their classmates.

Keep Going

Have the children use the tortoise body as a template for another page on which they can write a short story of their own.

Book Break

Look Out for Turtles! by Melvin Berger (Econo-Clad Books, 1999). A lovely presentation of comprehensive turtle information, including how they've survived millions of years and why they're threatened now.

Komodo Dragons & Mice

(Crafts, Language Arts)

Children assemble puppets for a play about the Komodo dragon's eating habits.

You'll Need

Komodo Dragon and Mouse Puppets (page 27) ◎ "Of Mice and Menus" read-aloud play (page 28) ◎ paste ◎ scissors ◎ paint and brushes ◎ oaktag ◎ clear tape ◎ craft sticks ◎ old sponges ◎ metal bowls and spoons

Komodo dragons are known for their unpleasant dispositions. If there are no other animals around to assail, they'll fight with one another. In fact, they frequently make meals of each other! This king of the monitor lizards goes after—and often gets—animals as large as deer and horses. Komodos are the only sizable predator in their habitat (growing to more than 10 feet in length and weighing more than 220 pounds), so they're never picked on by someone their own size.

In this whimsical play, the reptilian bullies brag about imaginary encounters, only to be startled by tiny creatures that are tired of their boasting. Enlist children's help in creating the puppets for the play, which requires four mice and four Komodo dragons:

1. Make four copies of page 27. Cut out the mouse, Komodo dragon, and its legs.
2. Glue each mouse puppet to oaktag, then paint them and cut them out. Tape a craft stick to each back for easy handling.
3. Glue each Komodo puppet to oaktag. Paint the body and legs with a thin mixture of green and brown paint. While the paint is wet, blot it with a sponge or crumpled paper towel to give it a lizard-like texture.
4. When the paint on the Komodo puppets is dry, cut slits along the dotted lines on the body and legs. Slip the leg tabs into the slits, as shown.

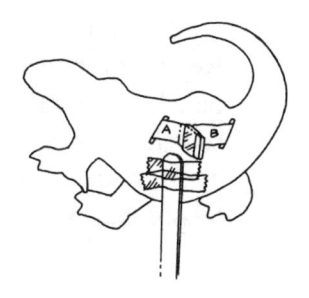

Remarkable Reptiles 17

5. Tape a craft stick to the backside of each lizard. Tape tabs A and B together, as shown. When the taped tabs are wiggled up and down, the legs will move. Now the Komodo is ready to perform!

The play's dialogue is made up of one-line rhymes, easy for students to memorize and act out using their puppets. Children will love how the underdogs in this play win a round!

Keep Going

Have students check the "Reptile Resources" for pictures of the Komodo's Indonesian habitat. Have them paint a backdrop setting for the play.

Daily Reptile Reporter
(Science, Critical Thinking)

Children read fascinating facts about reptiles and play fun games.

You'll Need

Daily Reptile Reporter (page 30)   pencils

Make a photocopy of the Daily Reptile Reporter for each student. They'll read a bunch of fun facts about reptiles, play a word-search game, and count a jumble of snakes. Then, students can test their reptile-savvy by taking the "Slithery Fact Quiz."

Answers

Jumbled Snakes: 7
Slithery Facts Quiz: 1. True   2. False
3. True   4. False   5. False   6. False
7. True   8. True   9. False   10. True

Book Break

Hide and Snake by Keith Baker (Voyager Picture Books, 1995). Find the sneaky snake that's hiding in a series of intricate drawings.

Teaching With the Poster
(Mapping Skills, Critical Thinking)

Students read a map to learn about five reptiles and their homes.

You'll Need

"A World of Reptiles" poster   globe

The poster features five remarkable reptiles from around the world, along with some interesting bits of information. Point out the different places where the reptiles live. Then show children a globe and have them locate the same places on the globe. Invite children to quiz each other about the reptiles featured in the poster.

Remarkable Reptiles

Name _____

What Am I? Animal Maze

Pick one of the animals below. Then follow the maze to find out if your animal is a reptile, amphibian, or mammal.

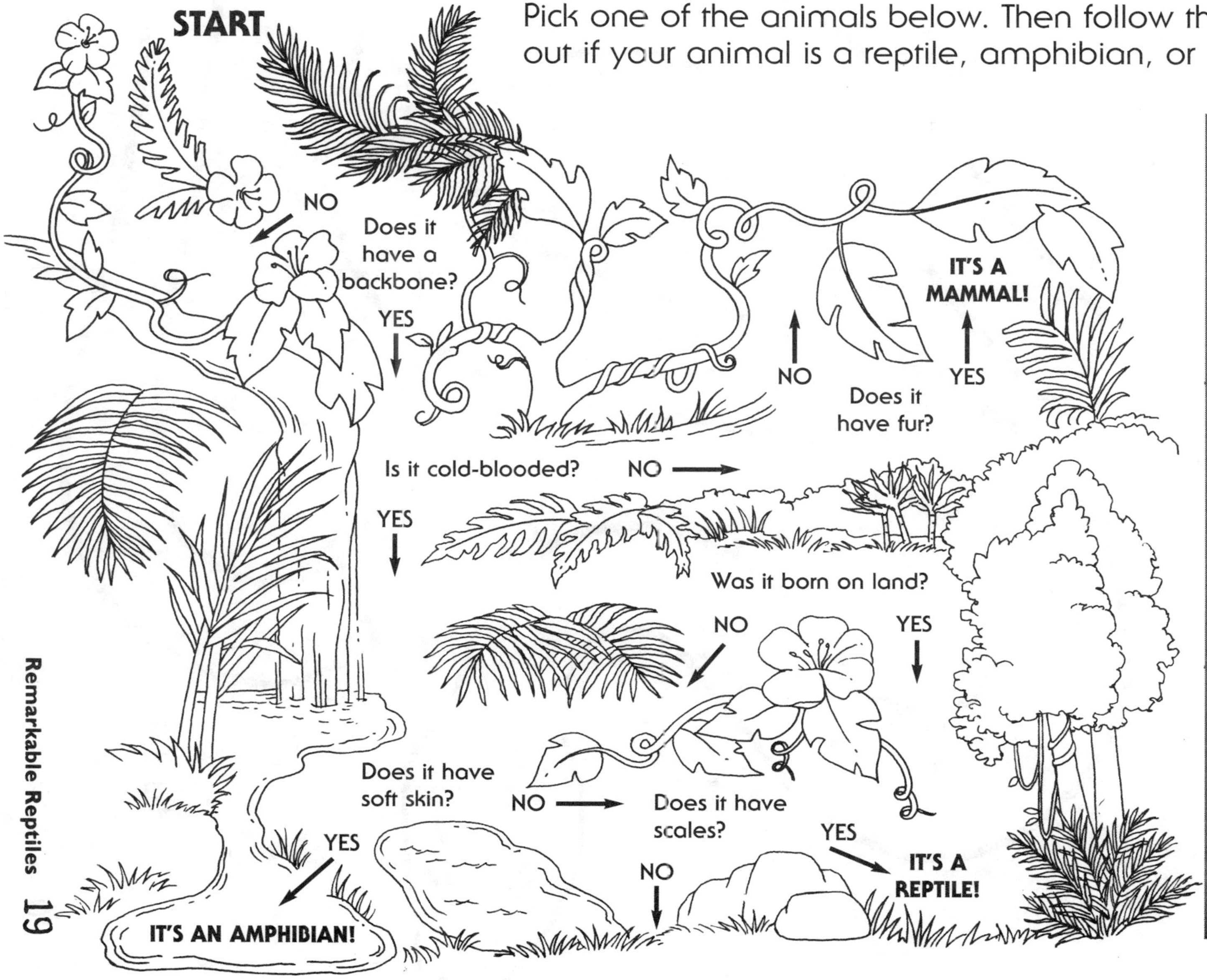

Frog
- has a backbone. 
- is cold-blooded.
- was born in water.
- has soft skin.

Monkey
- has a backbone.
- is warm-blooded.
- was born on land.
- has fur.

Rattlesnake
- has a backbone.
- is cold-blooded.
- was born on land.
- has scales.

START

Does it have a backbone? NO

YES →

Is it cold-blooded? NO ↑

YES →

Was it born on land? YES →

NO

Does it have fur? YES → **IT'S A MAMMAL!**

NO ←

Does it have scales? YES → **IT'S A REPTILE!**

NO →

Does it have soft skin? YES → **IT'S AN AMPHIBIAN!**

Remarkable Reptiles 19

Design a Snake

What's your favorite kind of snake? Color this snake to look like your favorite snake. Write the snake's name on the label below.

Label ➔

20 **Remarkable Reptiles**

Albert the Alligator

Cut out the alligator and its "scutes."
Write two questions about alligators on the blank scutes.
Then, write the answers on the alligator's body.

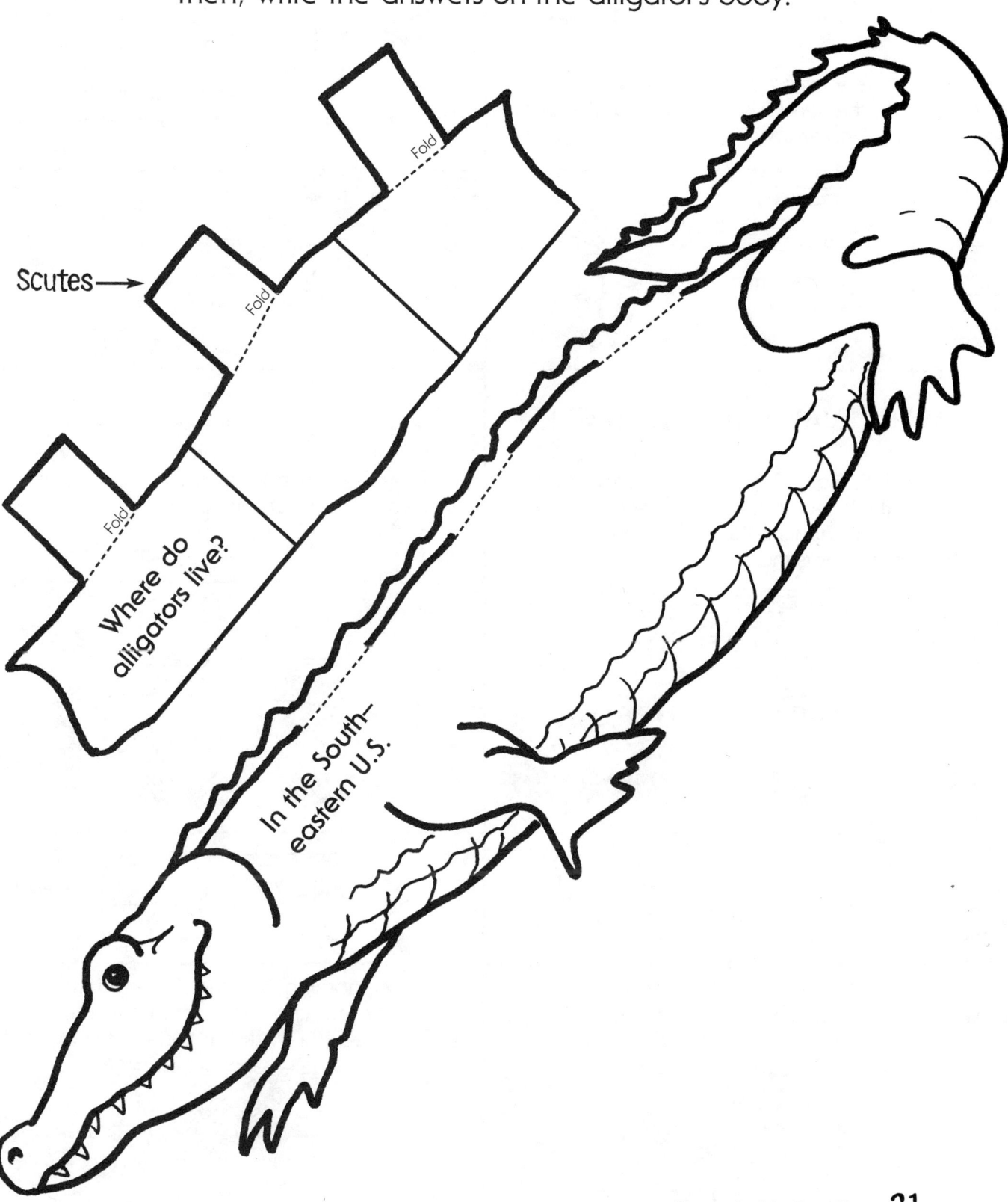

Scutes →

Fold

Where do alligators live?

In the South-eastern U.S.

Remarkable Reptiles 21

Sea Turtle Mini-Book

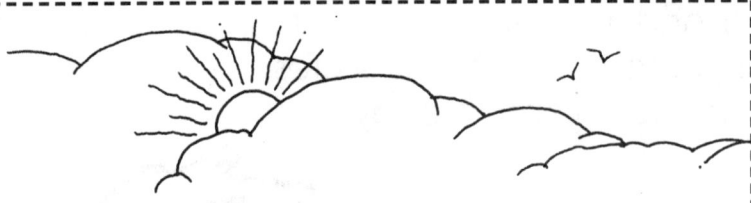

The turtle's eggs are hidden safely. The sun heats up the sand. Under the sand, the eggs stay nice and warm.

They made it! Most of the baby turtles swim in the ocean. They will live and grow in the water for many, many years. Someday, a few will return to the beach to lay their own eggs.

MAKE WAY FOR SEA TURTLES!

On a dark night, a mother sea turtle crawls out of the ocean. She digs a deep hole in the beach. Then she lays her eggs in the hole and covers them with sand.

In a few months, the baby turtles are ready to hatch. They use a special egg beak to help break out of their shells.

The baby turtles are out! They head for the water. Hungry birds fly toward the babies. They try to catch some turtles for food.

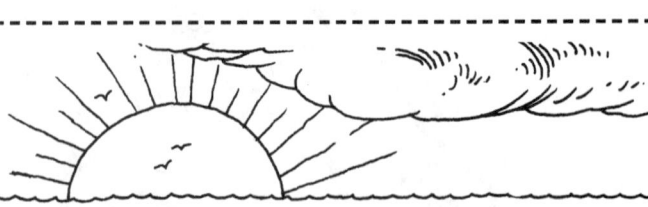

The next morning, the mother sea turtle is gone. She has crawled back into the sea. You can see her tracks on the sand.

Python Patterns

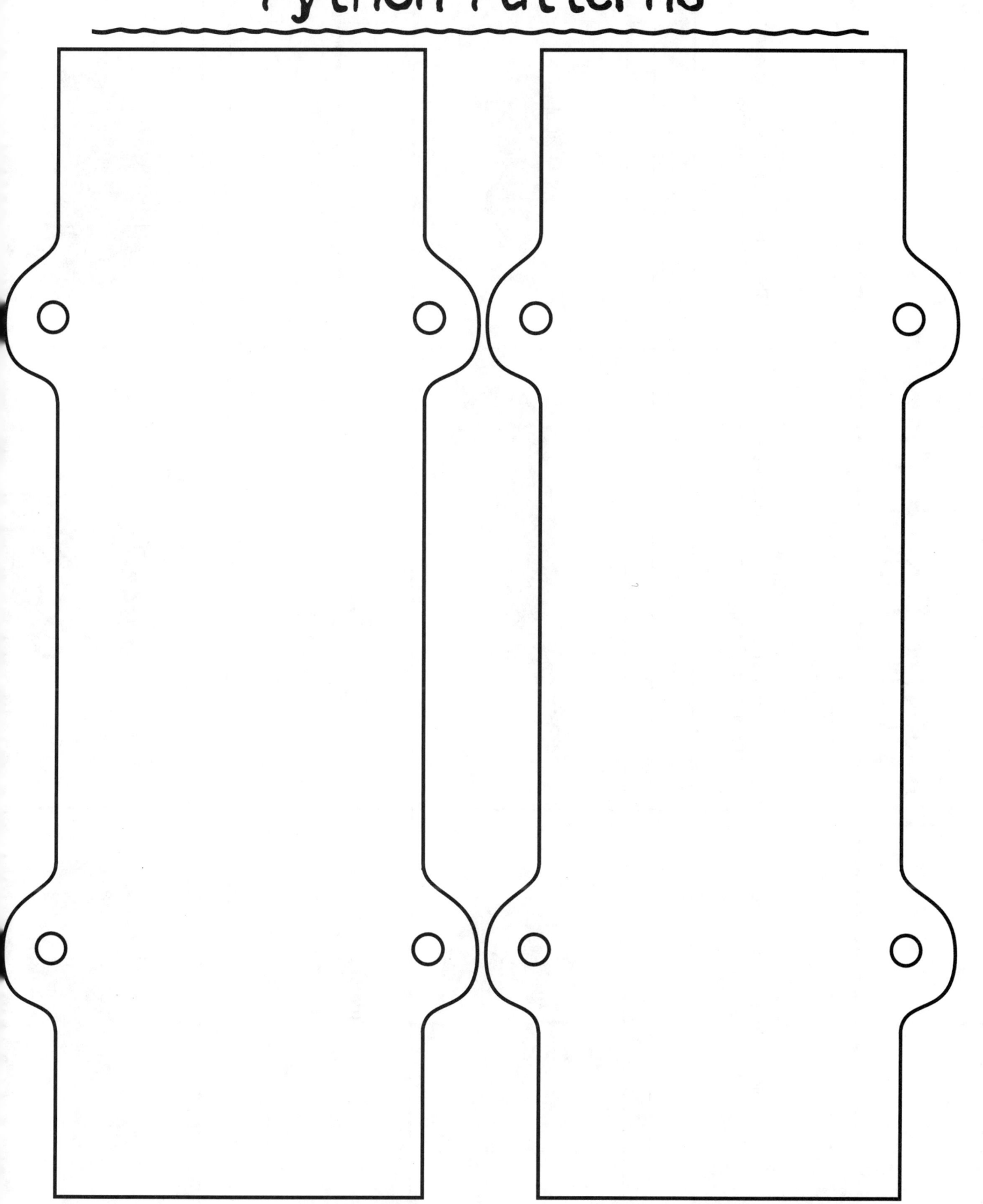

Remarkable Reptiles 23

Reptile Fact Cards

Matamata
This turtle doesn't bite or chew.
It sucks up its meals.
_____
_____

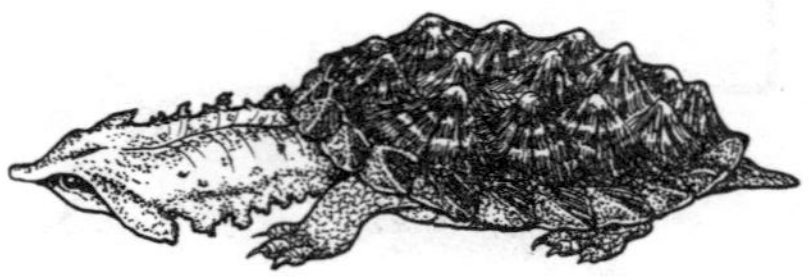

Chameleon
This lizard can look in two directions at the same time.
_____
_____

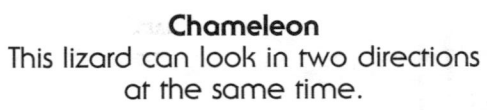

Gharial
This crocodile swallows stones to help digest, or break down, its food.
_____
_____

Rattlesnake
This snake doesn't lay eggs.
It gives birth to live young.
_____
_____

Marine Iguana
This reptile is the only lizard that lives in the sea.
_____
_____

Tuatara
This one-of-a-kind reptile can live up to 120 years.
_____
_____

Reptile Fact Cards

Anaconda
This giant snake spends most of its time in water.

Alligator Snapping Turtle
This turtle has a very large head with a strong beak.

Komodo Dragon
This giant lizard eats deer, wild pigs, and other Komodo dragons.

Leatherback Turtle
This sea turtle likes to eat jellyfish and crabs.

Saltwater Crocodile
This crocodile can grow up to 23 feet long!

Giant Tortoise
This slow turtle would take a whole morning to cross a football field.

A Turtle's Tale

Hi!

My name is

_____.

I am a very _____

tortoise. I live near the

_____.

On sunny days I like to _____

with my _____. When I'm not

playing or _____, I'm

probably eating. My favorite

snack is _____.

Remarkable Reptiles

Komodo Dragon and Mouse Puppets

TAB
Komodo's front leg

TAB
Komodo's rear leg

Remarkable Reptiles 27

Of Mice and Menus

Read-Aloud Play

CAST:

Komodo Dragon #1
Komodo Dragon #2
Komodo Dragon #3
Komodo Dragon #4

Mouse #1
Mouse #2
Mouse #3
Mouse #4

PROPS:
4 metal dishes and spoons

SCENE: A clearing in an island forest. Four Komodo dragons appear, stomping and snorting. Four tiny mice, hidden in the shade of a tree, watch the dragons.

Komodo chorus: *(loudly)* .... We rule this whole island, far and near,
and everyone else trembles in fear!
We huff and we puff,
we hiss and we roar!

Mice chorus: .... Oh no, not again!
(rolling their eyes) We've heard this before.

Komodo #1: *(boastfully)* .... If I met a rhino,
I'd cook rhino pie!

Mouse #1: *(aside, to audience)* ...... If he saw a rhino,
he'd learn how to fly.

Komodo #2: *(boastfully)* .... If I met a crocodile,
I'd brew crocodile stew!

Remarkable Reptiles

Mouse #2: *(aside, to audience)* ..... This dragon, I fear,
        hasn't a clue.

Komodo #3: *(boastfully)* .... If I met a cheetah,
        I'd eat it with cream!

Mouse #3: *(aside, to audience)* ..... This silly dragon is having a dream.

Komodo #4: *(boastfully)* .... If I met a tiger,
        I'd gobble it rare!

Mouse #4: *(aside, to audience)* ..... If he met a tiger,
        he'd faint then and there.

Komodo #1: *(boastfully)* .... If I met a leopard,
        I'd broil leopard steak!

Mouse #1 *(aside, to audience)* ...... I wish these big bullies
        would give me a break.

Komodo #2: *(boastfully)* .... If I met a hippo,
        I'd bake hippo bread!

Mouse #2 *(aside, to audience)* ...... Surely this dragon
        fell on his head.

Komodo #3: *(boastfully)* .... If I met a lion,
        I'd make lion Jell-O!

Mouse #3 *(aside, to audience)* ...... This dragon, you see,
        is not a smart fellow.

Komodo chorus: .... We're dragons! We're tough!
(loudly, swaggering)   We're mean and we're rough!

Mouse #4 *(to other mice)* .... So what do you say?
        Have we heard enough?

(The mice all slowly nod "yes," and they all leap from behind the tree, banging their spoons on their metal bowls. The startled Komodos run away, squealing.)

Remarkable Reptiles

Name _____

Daily Reptile Reporter

Remarkable Reptile Records

Turtles: smallest — 4-inch bog turtle
largest — 6-foot leatherback

Snakes: smallest — 5-inch thread snake
largest — 33-foot python

Lizards: smallest — 1 1/2-inch Virgin Island gecko
largest — 10-foot Komodo dragon

Crocodiles: smallest — 4-foot dwarf crocodile
largest — 23-foot saltwater crocodile

Jumbled Snakes
How many snakes do you see?

Did You Know?

- Female snakes are almost always larger than males.
- Some snakes have 400 vertebrae, but humans have only 33.
- Geckos twitch their tails like cats before pouncing on prey.
- Fossils show that turtles used to have teeth.
- If you removed the lead from your pencil, a thread snake would fit in that empty space.
- An anaconda can swallow a whole wild pig.
- Some reptiles eat only three or four times a year.

- Land tortoises live in America, Africa, Asia, and Europe, but not in Australia.
- The king cobra is considered the most venomous snake in the world.
- Tuataras have one row of bottom teeth, but two rows of top teeth.
- Green sea turtles swim 1,400 miles to lay their eggs on Ascension Island.
- Chameleons can shoot out their tongues at the speed of a bullet.
- Puff adders burrow into the sand tail-first.
- Anacondas, pythons, and boas all have leftover tiny hind legs.

Remarkable Reptiles

Daily Reptile Reporter

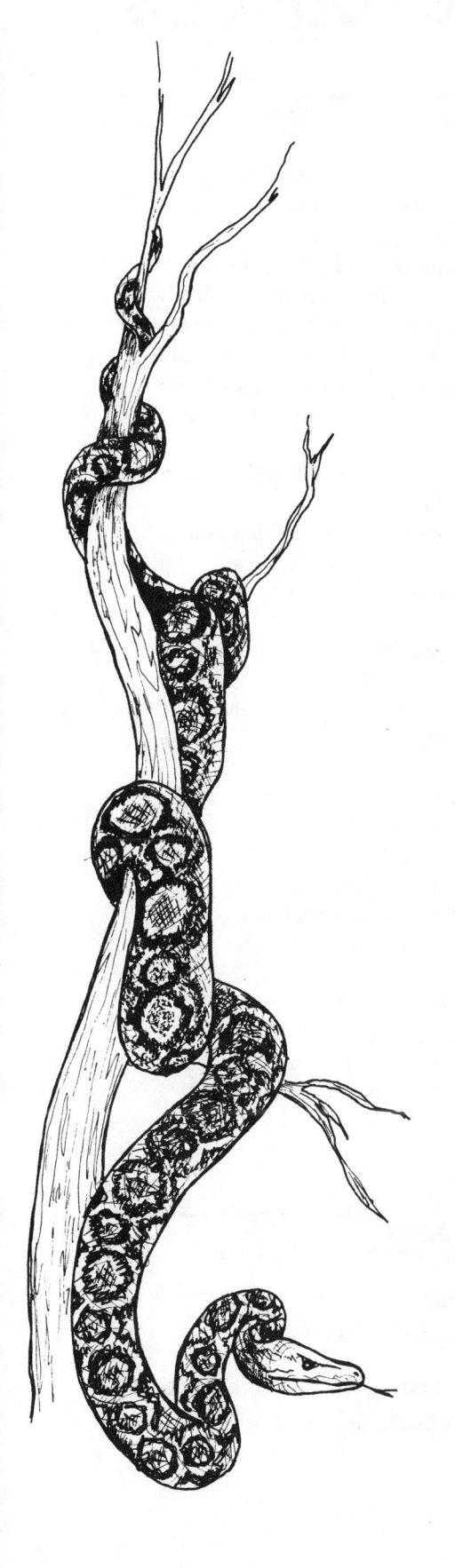

Reptile Detective

Find these 11 reptilian words hidden in the grid:

ALLIGATOR ◎ BOA ◎ GECKO ◎ GHARIAL
LIZARD ◎ PLATES ◎ SCALES ◎ SCUTES
SHELL ◎ SNAKE ◎ TURTLE

```
C D F J S L P Q R G S U T
B O A I N M O L W H V X U
E H G K A L L I G A T O R
Z S Y A K C N Z U R G I T
S C U T E S F A L I H K L
M A N B D E P R J A Q R E
P L A T E S S D T L U V X
A E B D C F Y E H G W I J
K S H E L L Z G E C K O L
```

Slithery Facts Quiz

How much do you really know about reptiles? Circle the correct answer.

True	False	1.	Snakes swallow their food whole.
True	False	2.	Turtles are warm-blooded.
True	False	3.	Some snakes give birth to live young.
True	False	4.	There are 350 kinds of tuataras.
True	False	5.	All turtles have webbed feet.
True	False	6.	A Komodo dragon is a kind of alligator.
True	False	7.	Snakes shed their skin a few times a year.
True	False	8.	Sea turtles lay their eggs on land.
True	False	9.	Boa constrictors are poisonous.
True	False	10.	Crocodiles can be more than 20 feet long.

Remarkable Reptiles

Reptile Resources

Books

Alligator Baby by Robert N. Munsch
(Cartwheel, 1997)
This story tells kids what happens when one girl's parents mistakenly bring home a baby alligator instead of a baby brother.

Chameleons Are Cool by Martin Jenkins
(Candlewick Press, 1998)
A boy enthusiastically describes chameleons—from their ability to change colors to how they see and hunt. Cool facts caption vivid watercolors.

Crocodiles & Alligators by Seymour Simon
(HarperCollins, 1999)
Seymour Simon's sharp eye zooms in to snap spectacular photos. Text explains how to tell crocodiles from alligators, where "crocodile tears" come from, and much more.

Gator or Croc? by Allan Fowler
(Children's Press, 1997)
Using simple text and color photographs, this book explains the difference (and similarities) between alligators and crocodiles.

The Hunterman and the Crocodile:
A West African Folktale by Baba Wague Diakite
(Scholastic, 1997)
What happens when Bamba the hungry Crocodile convinces Donso the Hunterman to carry his family to the river? Find out if Bamba has second thoughts about his promise not to eat the hunter in this beautifully portrayed tale.

Lyle, Lyle, Crocodile by Bernard Waber
(Houghton Mifflin, 1987)
This well-reviewed picture book follows the adventures of a New York City crocodile and his conflicts with the neighbor's cat.

The Mixed-Up Chameleon by Eric Carle
(HarperTrophy, 1988)
Find out what happens when a chameleon at the zoo finds out he can really change—he takes on the form of all the other zoo animals.

National Audubon Society First Field Guide:
Reptiles by John L. Behler (Scholastic, 1999)
Full-color photos complement basic information about North American reptiles and amphibians, including their physical characteristics, senses, metabolism, reproduction, and growth.

Outside & Inside Snakes by Sandra Markle
(Econo-Clad Books, 1999)
A question-and-answer format and spectacular photos will draw students in as they learn about nearly every aspect of a snake's life.

Slinky, Scaly Snakes! by Jennifer Dussling
(Dorling Kindersley, 1998)
Attention-grabbing photos, fun facts, and small blocks of copy make this book appealing and accessible to early readers.

S-S-Snakes by Lucille Penner
(Econo-Clad Books, 1999)
Illustrations and easy-to-follow text take you around the world of snakes. Check out snakes that fly and a species that spews blood!

3D Reptile by John A. Burton
(Dorling Kindersley, 1998)
This book comes with a mirror that "magically" turns the photos into awesome—and possibly alarming—3-D shots.

Web Sites

World of Reptiles
www.natureexplorer.com/WR/WR.html

Awesome Amphibians, Remarkable Reptiles
www.stlzoo.org/content.asp?page_name=herpfacts

Remarkable Reptiles